THE CARPENTER

THE CARPENTER

Carolyn I. Furlong

To order additional copies of this book, contact:
Xlibris Corporation
1-888-795-4274
www.Xlibris.com
Orders@Xlibris.com
46116

Contents

*This book
is dedicated
to the
McElroy Cousins.*

Acknowledgements

The following have provided
invaluable assistance
in the preparation of this book:

Bill and Lucille McElroy

Bettina J. Speyrer

Willard F. Whitaker, III

The Holy Bible
The Book Of Ecclesiastes
Chapter 1:3-11

What do people gain from all the toil
at which they toil under the sun?
A generation goes, and a generation comes,
but the earth remains forever.
The sun rises and the sun goes down,
and hurries to the place where it rises.
The wind blows to the south, and goes around to the north;
round and round goes the wind,
and on its circuits the wind returns.
All streams run to the sea, but the sea is not full;
to the place where the streams flow,
there they continue to flow.
All things are wearisome; more than one can express;
the eye is not satisfied with seeing, or the ear filled with hearing.
What has been is what will be,
and what has been done is what will be done;
there is nothing new under the sun.
Is there a thing of which it is said,
"See, this is new?"
It has already been, in the ages before us.
The people of long ago are not remembered,
nor will there be any remembrance
of people yet to come by those who come after them.

Prologue

The flames could be seen from miles away. The old frame farmhouse, once the sparks from the stove flew from the chimney and ignited the dried leaves on the roof, did not have a chance. One of the grown daughters who was at home began throwing her sisters' good coats from the upstairs window, until the smoke drove her outside. The neighbors came as fast as they could hitch their teams to the wagons. Two of them lifted the buffet and carried it to the front yard, thus saving the wife's good dishes. Time ran out as the timbers came crashing down and not much else could be saved.

One neighbor who had an almost new 1932 8-cylinder Ford drove to the schoolhouse with news of the fire. The teacher was the second oldest daughter of the farmer whose house had burned. Two of the students were her younger sisters. The youngest began to cry and the teacher took the 6-year-old child onto her lap. The other nine students in the one-room school went pale and silent. The smell of smoke filled their nostrils as the fire, two miles away, crackled a few more times and then died.

Chapter One

Carl straightened his back and inspected the site where he was going to build the house. All evidence of the fire had been removed. The yard was clean and smooth, except for the eight-foot deep excavation that was to be the basement. He felt a sense of excitement mixed with dread that came and went as he tried to avoid thinking of the hard work ahead of him. Take it one day at a time, Carl thought.

An ancient wooden chest of tools sat nearby. A few had been retrieved from the ashes following the fire and others had been borrowed from his brother. His brother had also helped him draw plans for the house, which was to be two stories with a full cement basement. Two windows equal in size would face the road and in the middle he would build a small stoop. The front door might have a glass window, depending on how much the lumber yard wanted for it when he got around to the door. The blueprints were not at the farm but were safe in the furnished house the wife had rented when the old house burned. He did not need them, anyway, because he had memorized every detail.

As he stood in thought, Carl said to himself as he had hundreds of times that he was not cut out to be a farmer. Carl hated farming and his life as a farmer so intensely that it filled his soul. His face reflected his bitterness and rage more often than not. He was a carpenter, damn it! A carpenter and a damn good one! Carl and his brother had built nearly half of the houses in Blakesville, where he and the wife lived for the first few years of their marriage and where their first three girls were born. Everyone had admired those houses, Carl recalled, no two alike and each one built to withstand the Iowa tornados and ice storms. It made him feel good to think of those houses. The new house was going to be even better. It was going to have plenty of windows and an open stairway at one end of the living room. The wife would like that.

The sound of a car approaching broke into his reverie. He listened for a moment as it neared the bridge down the road. Thwack. Thump. It was on the bridge now and slowed down as it rumbled across. Very few cars used this road and Carl recognized the sound of the motor. It was the mail man. They called it the Rural Free Delivery, RFD for short. The farm was on RFD No. 4, which is how his mail was addressed. Carl knew the mail man's name but not much else. There was never time to talk but Carl did not mind. While the weather permitted, the mail man had to get on with his route on those roads that had no gravel. Carl did not care about any of this because all he wanted was the paper. The newspaper was his lifeline, the most precious thing in his day. Before the old house burned, when he was in the cornfield, he would use the excuse that he needed a drink of water from the well when the mail man came. He admitted that his heart always beat a little faster as he anticipated reading the news. Carl's expression relaxed as he recalled his neighbor, a Swede, who pronounced it "noose". "What's the noose?" the Swede would ask. Damn fool.

The mail man did not wait for Carl to reach the roadside mailbox. He simply tossed the paper inside and chugged away. "What the hell?" Carl thought, glancing at the cloudless sky. Unfriendly devil. He settled with the paper under a tree in what had once been their front yard. An end of old rope wound around a branch that had held the girls' swing. Carl turned the pages, looking in vain for something about President Roosevelt. Maybe tomorrow. Carl carefully placed the paper under a rock and rose painfully to his feet. Digging that basement with a pick axe and shovel had been hard work. He again approached the tool box, taking careful inventory. The truck from the lumber yard should be here soon, bringing the cement. It had to be mixed and spread on the floor of the gaping basement hole before it rained. The wife was usually accurate with her forecasts of rain. "Red sky at night, sailor's delight. Red in the morning, sailors take warning." She had not forecast any rain for the next week. Just in case, Carl thought he would check the paper, although it was yesterday's news.

Hell, it would be dark before he was done this day.

The election of Franklin Delano Roosevelt was a huge event in Carl's life. He had walked down the railroad track to the polls on a cold November day to vote for Roosevelt, his heart full of hope. The crash of '29 and the following years were extremely harsh, even for farmers who raised crops and livestock for their families' food. The price of hogs was a disaster, hardly covering their minimal feed and the price of the truck to take them to the packing house. It was a good thing that the wife could sew. Flour sacks and some chicken feed sacks that came in a printed material were used to make dresses for the girls. The fourth girl, now eleven, wore overalls like a boy. In fact, everyone called her "Carl's boy" as she liked to work alongside him. He had taken her on the plow when she was not much more than a baby. The sixth child was finally a boy but he was still small, only three. He was the last, Carl promised himself. As he paused to ponder these severely hard times, Carl realized that the children, even the older girls, did not feel that they were poor. In fact, it often appeared that they considered themselves luckier than most.

Carl remembered with excitement the night of Roosevelt's election. They were still in the old house and he had made sure that the battery for the radio was charged. He had hauled the battery, almost too heavy for one man to lift, to town in the wagon for it to be charged. He had also warned the girls not to run down the battery by playing the radio until after the election. They liked to come home from school and listen to Jack Armstrong, the All American Boy, and sing along with the sponsor: "have you t-r-i-i-e-e-d Wheaties, the best breakfast food in the l-a-a-n-n-d".

Carl had invited his best friend and neighbor, Doug, to come listen to the election returns with him. He could not recall exactly why, since Doug's farmhouse was wired for electricity. It was on a better, more traveled road where the county electric company had placed poles and strung wire. It may have been decided that Doug would come to his house because Doug had a car. He could get home quicker after the final returns were in. It was very late, well after midnight, when it was announced that Franklin D. Roosevelt would be the next president. Doug cheered along with Carl, although he leaned slightly toward Hoover, the Republican candidate. Carl tried to overlook this grave error of judgment because he did not want to argue with his friend. Doug was very good to Carl and his family, giving them a ride to town when they had money for shoes or groceries. The two often sat in the yard on the occasion of Sunday dinners, discussing politics and critiquing the leadership. Carl was radical in his love for Roosevelt and the Democrat party.

After the broadcast was over, Doug went out to crank his car and start the engine for the trip home. Carl blew out the lamp and groped his way to the stairway door, which was slightly open. On the bottom step he found a sleeping five-year-old, his youngest girl. He was not surprised. The little one always seemed to be reading his mind. She hardly ever spoke to him directly and hung her head when she asked a rare question. However, he was aware that she had sensed his anticipation of the election. He guessed that she was curious and wanted to hear for herself what the excitement was all about. Carl picked her up and climbed the stairs to return her to the bed she shared with her sister. He made a silent promise that tomorrow he would try to modify his gruff tone, for her benefit, at least. Carl went to bed with a feeling of great relief and optimism now that Roosevelt was elected. If he had believed in God, he would have almost said a prayer of thanks.

The cement delivery was uneventful. The man from the lumber yard wanted to talk, but Carl let him know he had to get to work. He was already preparing the first batch of cement as he heard the departing truck thwack thump over the bridge. To take his mind off the job facing him, he wondered what might be different if the county electric company should string wires on his road. Carl knew that would never happen but still, he tried to imagine a machine, powered by electricity or a motor of some kind, which would mix the cement. Chastising himself for having foolish dreams, Carl pumped a bucket of water from the well. He poured it carefully into the tub of cement, then took up the old shovel with its broken handle and began to mix.

Chapter Two

All of the vertical two by fours were in place, standing like a small army of soldiers. The empty spot where the old house had stood was miraculously filling up. Carl looked around with satisfaction at how much he had accomplished. There had not been a lot of rain to slow him down. This was very serious for the farmers who depended on the rain for their corn and wheat, but Carl had not planted any crops this year. He hoped to hell that the loan from the bank would hold out until he could sell the calves or hogs. The days were getting cool and he knew he had to get the house closed in before bad weather. Once it started to snow and freeze, he would work inside laying the floor and building the kitchen cabinets. Very few farm kitchens had built-in cabinets, although he had helped Doug build cabinets in his house. Doug and his wife had a nice house and a nice car. They had two boys who were good as any hired hand and a little one near the same age as his own. Carl quickly changed his thoughts to quell the familiar twinge of envy. He thought a lot of his neighbor and friend Doug. He just wished that Doug was a little more of a carpenter instead of so clumsy with a hammer.

His own grip on the handle of his hammer was skillful and true. No missed or bent nails. He handled his level and plane with equal skill. Hell, he was a carpenter. What else could anyone expect? Carl also reflected that it took more than a steady hand. Building a house took intelligence. He liked the word "in-tell-i-gence" and said it out loud, knowing that it was something he possessed. You had to have a good head on your shoulders and you had to concentrate on that one section of the whole picture.

Carl did not exactly look down on the man at the bank, one of the few businessmen he had ever met. He conceded that the banker had to know his customers, who he could trust to pay back the loan and who he could not, but let the poor devil try to build a house.

Carl decided to take a break. His right hand went automatically to the pocket in the bib of his overalls and drew out a crumpled pack of Beech Nut tobacco. Red and yellow Beech Nut tobacco packages littered the entire farm, to the most remote corners of the pasture. Two fingers dipped into the bag and placed a large pinch of the tobacco directly onto his tongue. He savored it and sucked the sharp juice down his throat. Peering inside the bag, he hoped the store across from the house they rented would be open in the morning. He needed to get a new package before he started his walk down the railroad track to the farm. Carl usually felt good in the morning. The challenge and delight of a day with his tools and the pungent smell of new lumber made all the hard work worthwhile.

Now the days were getting somewhat shorter and it was growing dusk sooner. The milk cows had moseyed in from the pasture and were gathering at the gate outside the barn lot. Their udders were full and they switched their tails back and forth, nodding their heads as they chewed their cud. Carl used an oily rag to wipe his tools clean before replacing them in the wooden chest. The tool box was almost like a small casket, but with several bins the exact size of the tool it would hold. An old man in Blakesville had given it to him and his brother for hauling it off in their wagon. Finished with the tools for today. Now it was time to milk the cows and slop the hogs. Christ almighty! How had he ever let the wife talk him into buying this poor excuse for a farm? He knew the answer all too well, having rehearsed the argument in his mind for many years. "Mama and Papa will be mad if we don't buy the farm so they can move to town", Carl mimicked the wife's voice. He did not really mind milking the cows, because he knew it relieved them and besides, the little kids needed the milk. But milking cows and slopping hogs was not any kind of life for a carpenter. Hell no. Not this one, anyway.

It was nearly dark as Carl walked up the track with the bucket of milk. When it became too heavy, he put it down for a moment and looked up to see a new moon. The new moon was just a sliver and was almost lying on its back. The wife always said this position meant it was going to catch some rain, but there was no forecast for rain. Christ, he was tired.

Carl and his family had been lucky to find a house to move into the same night as the fire. Word had got around fast and a furnished house was located for ten dollars a month. The owner had moved in with his elderly parents who needed help temporarily. The house was almost directly across the road from a small store and close to the railroad depot. Since very little had been saved from the rapidly burning house, the wife said over and over that this was God's blessing.

The kerosene lamp was lit and sat in the middle of the oilcloth that covered the kitchen table. The two girls were studying under another lamp in the next room. Their sister who had taught at their school last year was now teaching at a larger school fifty miles away. She had a room within walking distance of the school and did some cooking and sewing for the family she lived with in exchange for the room. She was also helping her sister, the third daughter, finish high school. Carl had heard that she had a boy-friend, the son of a dairy farmer close to town. The boy-friend had a Chevy and his dad had a new Packard. Good! They might not have to depend on Doug every time they needed something from town. The wife would have to ask, though, as Carl was way too proud.

Carl gingerly eased his weary body into the rocking chair while the wife poured the milk into jars and put them in the ice box. They had not had an ice box in the old house. The man who delivered the ice said the road was too unreliable for regular deliveries. The wife liked having an ice box for keeping the milk cool. The cream would rise to the top by morning. She would use it for their oatmeal.

The wife began to warm his supper, corn bread and soup beans. She had flavored the beans with a bit of bacon, saved from the last time they had butchered a pig. He hoped that she had an onion left from the summer's garden. Corn bread and beans with a little onion on top was his favorite. The wife was a good cook and kept a clean neat house. For once, Carl forgot her treachery at talking him into buying that damn farm. He was too tired to worry any more about it.

The little boy toddled up and grabbed his knee, looking up expectantly. Carl pulled him onto his lap and began to sing in a low voice, "Gently oh gently, time in thy flight, make me a child again just for tonight."

Chapter Three

Fall weather had set in about when expected. The house was completely closed in and the windows were solidly in the frames that Carl had carefully measured. His brother was known for his skill at making windows and had brought them to the farm. They were a perfect fit. Only the three doors, one on each side of the house except the north, remained to be hung for the outside to be finished. Carl wanted to wait until closer to finishing to see if he had enough money left for the ones with glass. Makeshift board enclosures stood in the openings to keep out the cold. The furnace had not yet been installed in the basement. The truck would bring it as soon as there was a long enough freeze to guarantee that the road would be passable. Carl had decided against running the heat ducts to the upstairs. Anyway, the heat could go up the open stairway. The wife's brother had a truck and made his living in the wintertime hauling coal. There were a number of mines in the surrounding countryside and coal was cheap. Dirty, though. "Black as coal" was everyone's expression since coal furnaces began replacing wood-burning stoves.

The cows and the two horses could no longer graze in the pasture, now brown and dead. This meant bringing pitchforks of hay and buckets of corn from the barn, cutting into his time to work on the house. The days were short and Carl had to make the most of the daylight hours.

The downstairs bedroom was framed in. It could be used for either a bedroom or a dining room, as it was next to the kitchen. However, with six children Carl doubted it would ever be used for anything but a bedroom. The two upstairs bedrooms were partially completed. The upstairs was accessed by makeshift steps and a ladder, as the open stairway with a shiny wood railing that Carl envisioned had not yet taken shape. A long closet ran along the north side of the upstairs, with access from each bedroom. Carl was not satisfied with the height of the closet which was under the eaves of the sloping roof, but hell it would be a good place for the little kids to play when it rained. Carl would build a hall between the two bedrooms, which he hoped would be a buffer for sound. He was so damn tired of those kids coughing half the night. How could a man sleep with that noise going on? Yelling at them to stop did no good.

Carl began to wonder when his bad temper had started. He had not always been that way and he was ashamed. As he hammered nail after nail, relishing the shiny newness of their steel, his thoughts went back to when he first knew the wife. He was happy-go-lucky in those days. She was only eighteen but already teaching school. Teachers were not required to have any particular education then, in 1908, but she had a teaching certificate from the county. In his mind, she was so lovely. Not just pretty, she was lovely in every way. Her dark hair curled around her sweet face. He wanted to get to know her the first time he laid eyes on her. It was in the church basement on the occasion of the pie supper. They had a little game where the girls and women baked a pie and wrote their name on the bottom of the tin pan. The older boys and men selected a pie and got to eat it with the one who had baked it. He had not actually picked her pie but some swapping took place and they got to sit together. Carl recalled that he had asked if he could take her home in his buggy, but she said mama would not allow it. Girls were not supposed to be alone with boys. Still, something in her expression told him that she liked him. He had not thought much about it, but his wavy hair was very black and his features clean cut and handsome. The clothes he wore to church were as good as or better than those worn by the other young men looking for potential wives. Only his brother knew that Carl was stuck on her.

Although they lived some distance apart, Carl always looked for her on other occasions. The area was very social in the four or five months of good weather. There were covered dish dinners in the church basement, picnics on the school ground and Sunday afternoons when visiting a neighbor meant making ice cream. This required owning an ice cream freezer and someone going to town for a cake of ice. Then the women would skim the heaviest cream off the top of the milk, put in just enough sugar and a spoon of vanilla. The men's job was taking an axe or an ice pick to the cake of ice until the pieces were fine enough to fit into the freezer around the container of cream. The boys had a contest to see who could turn the freezer handle faster so the ice cream would be ready sooner. Sometimes there was a fresh angel food cake to go with it.

Carl had opportunities to see her on these occasions as well as during wheat harvesting time, when the neighbor boys joined the men to form a threshing crew. The women got together to cook a huge dinner at noon, usually fried chicken, but sometimes pork chops, again requiring someone to go to town for the meat. The men came to the house at noon on the dot. They took off their caps and washed up beside the well where a wash stand stood with soap and a towel. One by one, each pumped water into the wash pan, rubbed soap briskly onto his hands and splashed water on his face. The wash pan was then emptied onto the grass and the process was repeated by the next man. When all had washed they filed in to take their places at the table. The women always outdid themselves, trying to set a better spread than her neighbor for the previous threshing crew. In addition to the fried chicken or pork chops, there was always homemade bread, butter churned from yesterday's cream, mashed potatoes and gravy, vegetables from the late summer garden and pie baked with apples from the orchard. This was washed down with plenty of cold sweetened tea. The girl did not meet Carl's eyes when she went around the table with the pitcher of tea, but the tugging in his stomach told him she knew he was there.

One warm early May night Carl felt he could stand it no longer. He did not attend the Sunday night church service because he liked it or was religious, but he had been going for months on the chance that he could take her home. Once again, he approached her. Carl felt his cheeks burn when she told him that mama had agreed. At last! The horse was tied to a pole outside and a blanket was tucked in the buggy. They started down the main road in case someone was watching and then took a side road to a spot Carl had found a while ago. Without a word, he took her hand and helped her down. He had the blanket and she squeezed his hand as they climbed through the wire fence.

Chapter Four

When Carl awoke in the bedroom of the rented house, his first thought was whether he would be able to get up. The wife was already up and he could smell the coffee simmering on the stove. Damn, she was a good soul! For the past four days she and the girls had gone to the farm to milk the cows and do the chores. Carl admitted that he had not felt good for some time but not being able to work on the new house was something he had never anticipated.

It was not just the terrible tiredness but along had come the trouble with his bowels. What in hell was it? Everything he ate went right through him, and he had noticed the frequent redness. Carl recalled plowing the corn field when the urge came over him. He had to get off the plow and go right there in the field. The house had a toilet in the back yard but after dark the girls used a slop jar in the kitchen. He wondered sometimes if he would be able to make it to the toilet. What if he had to use the slop jar? No! Never!

There was a doctor in Blakesville but Carl dismissed the idea of trying to see her. She probably only knew how to deliver babies, anyway. He did not know anyone who had a doctor for any other reason. She had come to the old house to deliver all three of the little kids, bringing a bottle of whiskey for the wife in case she ran into trouble. But the wife had not needed it and he doubted if she would have taken a sip anyway. She did not believe in drinking whiskey. That was one reason why she did not like to see his brother come to visit. His brother usually had a bottle of whiskey in his car and all hell broke loose if he offered Carl a drink.

Carl's feet hit the cold floor and he groped for his overalls. Pulling them on, he noticed that they were very loose. He had lost more weight, which he could not spare. He would try to eat some of the wife's biscuits which he knew were waiting in the warm kitchen. Carl was determined to work on the house today. The wife said she would come to help with the chores as soon as the girls were home from school. The girls could keep the boy company and start supper.

Carl noticed the worried expression on the wife's face. He supposed she loved him, but God how could she? His gut had bothered him for so long and there was his bad temper. Christ, he was only 50. He had to beat this thing!

Chapter Five

Once Carl gripped the familiar handle of the hammer, he felt his strength come back. There was some urgency to finishing the house. The oldest girl wanted to come home to be married in the country church of her childhood. She had found a job teaching school in a town near Chicago but had to keep the wedding a secret. School teachers were not allowed to be married. She was determined to invite people to their home afterward. Carl knew he could not finish all the trim but felt sure the house would be presentable by the date of the wedding. They could move in a few weeks beforehand and the wife would have time to make curtains and furnish the living room. She had already located what she called a Duncan Phyfe table. It had sides that folded down and leaves to extend it for at least ten people. It would sit under the window on the north side of the room opposite the stairs. The wife had crocheted a runner for the top of the shiny table when it was not in use.

Carl did not feel much joy in going out of his way to satisfy the girl's request. She was born with red hair, a throw-back to her great-grandfather, which seemed to signal a rebellion that set her apart throughout school and to this very day. The second girl was placid and sweet, perhaps a little too eager to please. She was very generous. The third was also no trouble at all, in spite of unexplained seizures in her early years. Her eyesight was poor and she was still trying to finish high school. It had been eight years between the first three and the little kids coming along. Carl had waited all these years for a boy. That is not to say he did not love the girls, but hell, every man wants a son to carry on the family name.

Carl was not sure that the word "rebellion" was correct, but he did know that his oldest daughter had determination he did not see in many a boy. She left home when she was twelve, working for her room and board for some people in town so she could attend high school. She had also worked at the drugstore lunch counter when she got a little older. Then what did the damn fool do but decide to go to college! Carl shook his head in disbelief. A farm girl, going to college! He had taken the razor strap to her when she came home, but she ran out of the house and he could not catch her. She said she wanted to make something of herself, but hell, all those girls would end up doing would be working in someone's kitchen.

The time she had embarrassed him the most was at Doug's house once when she was home from college. When Carl and his family were invited to Sunday dinner, the women always stayed in the house, cooking dinner and discussing baking, canning or sewing. The girls stayed in the house, too, and made sure they were not caught looking out the window at the boys playing ball. The men talked politics in the yard, leaning against the car or sitting on the running board. What Hoover had not done for the country as opposed to what Roosevelt could do was a very serious discussion. That girl came right out and sat down with the men! She not only sat down as if she belonged there, but she started talking about what she had heard in college and what she had read in the paper. Carl could hardly control his temper but Doug motioned him that it was all right.

After the oldest girl went to Chicago to work at the 1932 Worlds Fair and look for a teaching job, she wrote to Carl that she would send him the fare to take the 300-mile train ride to see the city. It had a vast slaughter house area called the Chicago Stock Yards. Carl had never been out of the county where he was born, raised and now had a family. A train with only one passenger car, which the little kids called the Doodle Bug, stopped at the depot right up the track. It would take him to the station in town where a sleek new train, the Denver Zephyr, would take him into Chicago. However, on the day of departure there was a tremendous storm. Carl took this as a sign that he should not go and refused all future offers to see Chicago.

Another reason that he did not relish the upcoming wedding plans was that it reminded him of his own wedding. The father of the girl he was stuck on had come to him and coldly reported that she was in the family way. Carl resented the man's self-righteous demeanor. The father stated that a wedding would be held at their farm home as soon as proper arrangements could be made and the newspaper notified. A nice article on the society page of the paper was very important so that the marriage would not appear to be what some called a shotgun wedding. The ceremony took place in the very house that had recently burned to the ground, the old home of mama and papa.

Carl could not believe his incredible good fortune at having this lovely creature become his bride, but he did not appreciate the silly wedding plans. She was the oldest of three sisters and the other girls seemed to him to be foolish people, affected, not down to earth, more interested in what they should wear than what their futures would hold. Damn fools.

A baby on the way! Carl was excited beyond words but did not like the rigmarole that stood between him and having that precious girl for his wife. He vowed to take care of her for the rest of his life. He hoped that it would be a long one.

Chapter Six

At midday, Carl paused to open his thermos of coffee and briefly warm his hands. He squatted down and leaned against a two by four for a moment's rest. In the sudden quiet after a morning of sawing and hammering, he noticed that the wind was picking up. It had been calm when he started his morning trip down the track and he had not given a thought to the weather all day. Now that he stopped to think about it, he recalled that the mailman had come by earlier than usual and appeared to be losing no time covering his route. Was there a weather forecast he did not know about? The wife was busy packing the girls' dinner buckets when he left the house and had not given him her customary weather report.

The gusts of wind kept up a steady whistle under the eaves. Carl peered out the dusty window panes. To his surprise, he noticed that the cows and the two horses were waiting near the barn door, their heads down. Livestock, chickens and birds had some way of sensing when a storm might be coming. Still, Carl waited to collect his thoughts. A chew of tobacco would help him think.

After a few moments Carl picked up his cap and pulled it down over his ears. He decided the first thing he would do would be to gather the eggs. He discovered that he had worn only one coat this morning. Normally in very cold weather he wore a jacket under his rough wool coat, but hours earlier the weather turning nasty had been the farthest thing from his mind. Hell's fire!

The door of the chicken house was slamming in the wind. Carl went inside and felt in the nests for eggs but it was too early. The hens were huddled together, some in their nests but others in a corner. He groped on a shelf for the chicken feed sack and poured some cracked corn into the feeder before leaving. Carl carefully latched the door and double checked that it was secure.

The first flecks of icy moisture struck Carl's face as he made his way to the barn. Once the double doors were swung open, the horses went to their stalls and the cows to their mangers to be milked. The pigs were grunting and rooting in a small pile of hay. Carl threw several handfuls of corn in their direction and doled out some oats in buckets for the horses. He took up the clean milk can that the wife sent with him each morning. The cows did not have much milk, it being considerably earlier than usual. Finally, his chores done, Carl stood still for a moment looking at the silent livestock, which seemed to be staring back at him in the gloom. What more could he do? After closing and latching the barn doors, Carl carried the milk pail to the house to decide his next move. The wind-driven sleet was coming down hard now and froze on his coat as soon as it hit. The force of the wind was much stronger than when he had entered the barn. Some decisions had to be made, and quickly. It was already getting dark, although Carl calculated that it could not be much more than four o'clock. He wondered if the teacher had let school out early today. Hell no, Carl thought, it would take weather a lot worse than this for that damn school to close one minute before four o'clock. He could not recall it ever closing early.

Carl felt dizzy when he entered the house and sat down on a pile of boards. He realized he had not eaten since morning. The remaining coffee was ice cold but a piece of corn bread settled his stomach and he felt some strength return. He was tempted to just lie down and fall asleep. The house began to feel almost warm, once he was inside from the blizzard.

Blizzard? Yes, it could be called a blizzard, Carl conceded. The wind howled with maniacal force around the house. He congratulated himself that the sturdy walls, although not yet plastered, did not let in any wind at all. The old house had any number of spots around windows and doors where you could feel the wind. Carl thought back on the old house. He remembered several winters when the snow drifts covered the windows, so that he could not tell if it was morning or still the dead of night. The girls always amazed him that they went to school regardless of snow drifts. Sometimes it would thaw a little and then freeze, so that they could walk on the ice that formed on top of the drifts. The little boy would be starting to school in another year or so. His sister would help him through the snow drifts, Carl was sure.

Carl suddenly jolted wide awake and alert. He had to get the hell out of here before he froze to death. He thought of the wife's warm kitchen and in his mind's eye saw her glancing out the window, assessing the storm. Christ! What if she started out after him? Damn fool, it would be just like her!

Carl wasted no time getting ready to brave the wind and driving sleet. He decided he could not carry the milk, which he knew would be frozen over in a very short time. Out the back door he went, hoping against hope that it would stay light long enough for him to find his way to the railroad. His route up the lane and across the field to the creek was a short cut, but he knew he could never find his way in pitch black darkness. He had tried that in good weather! You could not cross the creek in darkness. Too many rocks to climb down and he did not dare fall. One of his old horses had slipped a half-mile or so up the creek, and it took a team of horses and three men to pull it out. Then the horse had to be shot as he had broken a leg.

Carl was aware that he was trying to keep his mind busy and finally found himself safe on the other side of the creek; only a short way now to the track. Once he climbed up the embankment onto the unprotected rails, the wind hit him full force in the face. Bending over nearly double, he faced into the wind and moved forward. Step by slow step, he tried to make a little progress. Then he decided to go back down the embankment and take hold of the fence, to which he would cling and possibly make better time. This worked for a short distance but the dead weeds and branches were impossible to navigate. Carl climbed back up onto the track and doubled over again to face the blizzard.

The youngest girl had told him once that it helped if she tried to sing in a bad storm. He didn't know why, but he thought of a neighbor who sang "Little Brown Church" in a very deep voice. "Little brown church in the wildwood, the little brown church in the dell. No spot is so dear to my childhood as the little brown church in the dell." You could hear the damn fool outside the church and down the road. Into Carl's mind drifted the words "Rock of ages, cleft for me, let me hide myself in thee" but he did not find any meaning in those words. He tried again. "On a hill far away stood an old rugged cross, the emblem of suffering and pain". Now, that was better. "And I'll love that old cross, where the dearest and best, for a world of lost sinners was slain". Good. "And I'll cherish the old rugged cross, 'til my trophies at last I lay down, I will cling to the old rugged cross, and exchange it some day for a crown." Lost in thought and with hymns filling his mind, Carl maintained slow but steady headway against the wind and icy sleet that was like nails being driven into his bare jaw. His steps became mechanical as his mind wandered.

Slowly returning to awareness, Carl thought he must be dying or even dead. The air was still and he opened his eyes to an eerie whiteness. It was snow! The sleet of so many hours had turned to snow! The early night air filled with snow flakes so quickly that they covered the shoulders and arms of his coat. His step was a little faster as he did not have to bend against the wind. He heard someone calling "Dad". "Dad?" "Dad!". He knew that voice. It was the third girl, living at home since finishing high school, come looking for him. Then he sighted the window of the house, which was lighted by the lamp, and the wife's face was pressed against the glass.

Carl found that he could move his stiff lips and whispered "*Thank you, God*".

Chapter Seven

Christmas was in the air. The little house seemed festive, with the aroma of fresh-baked mince meat pie cooling on the stove. There were no decorations, since all had burned in the old house; however, some pictures the girls had made with crayons in school were on display. Doug had given Carl a ride to town to buy English walnuts and an orange for each child, their traditional Christmas treat. These were in a cool hiding place awaiting Christmas morning. The second girl had written that she would be coming on the train Christmas Eve. She was bringing new mittens and scarves for the girls and a little toy train for the boy. A package from Chicago sent by the oldest girl was hidden in the closet. The girls were incredibly generous with what little they had. School teachers were not paid much. Fifty to eighty dollars a month was about average, and sometimes they were given tax warrants in lieu of money when the school district's funds were short.

Tonight was the night of the Christmas program. Carl wanted to forget about it but had agreed some years ago that this was the one occasion of the year that he would attend with the family. For the girls, the Christmas program was the social event of the year. It was held in the church rather than the small schoolhouse. Someone went to the church during the afternoon to fire up the furnace and warm the building. Others hung wreaths and decorated a tree that stood at one side of the sanctuary. A manger scene with a bale of hay and evergreen cuttings was on the other side. A fat red candle stood in each window, waiting to be lit just before the program started. Small brown paper bags had been filled with hard candy for distribution to each child at the end of their performance. The white frame church was always packed with family members and neighbors on this special night. The women brought pies for after the program and the aroma from the big coffee urn in the church basement was more than inviting.

Carl thought of Christmas before the old house burned. Times had not been so hard then. One year he had bought presents for everyone and had hid them in the barn until Christmas morning. He recalled the doll that said "mama" that he had bought for the fourth girl when she was eight years old. The boy was born just before that Christmas and her little sister was three. Carl felt sympathy for the eight-year-old who for several years had been the baby of the family, coddled by the wife and her older sisters. She had loved the doll and kept it in a safe place until three years later when it burned in the fire.

The wash pan was full of warm water and Carl stood in the kitchen, lathering his face with soap and preparing to shave. He sharpened the razor blade on the leather strap that hung from a nail. The wife was dressing the boy and helping the girls. They had secretly hoped for something new to wear, but it was not to be this year. Their sweaters had been handed down from the older girls as well as the skirts, which the wife had altered to fit. Their thick cotton stockings were clean and a fresh coat of brown polish had been applied to their everyday shoes. The third girl, in her late teens, planned to wear a felt hat that fit close over her ears. It had also previously belonged to the older girls and was said to be a flapper style. Carl did not know what the wife would wear, but she always looked pretty, even stylish. How did she do it? Not a woman in the county could compare to her fresh loveliness.

The evening was cold and there was snow on the ground, but the air was very still as the family started down the road. Carl carried the boy and the wife carried the pie. All wore their overshoes, which Carl hoped would last through the winter. The wife had been monitoring the almanac and reported that tomorrow would be the shortest day of the year. She also commented that as far back as she could remember it had never been bad weather on the night of the Christmas program. When they lived in the old house, they sometimes took the wagon or the buggy to the church, and once or twice had walked across the fields. On those occasions, the wife always said that it was "light as day". Indeed, the moon on the snow illuminated the night as light as day. This was one of those nights. There was no sound at all until the rumble of a distant freight train broke the silence.

The girls began to sing "It Came Upon a Midnight Clear", one of the carols in the program. They liked the new song "Santa Claus is Coming to Town", but it was considered too frivolous to be sung in the church. The eleven-year-old was to recite a piece, which she practiced as they walked up the road. They passed the homes of two or three neighbors, all with lamps in the windows. Carl wondered if they were not going to the Christmas program, an established neighborhood event. He pictured the inside of the warm little church. He knew that the church seemed large to the girls, but it did not compare to the churches he had worked on in Blakesville.

A neighboring farmer who was an artist had painted a portrait of Jesus that hung over the altar. On previous occasions, Carl had found it somewhat intimidating and had lowered his eyes rather than look too hard at the painting. A neighbor lady who could play the piano would be practicing the carols the children would sing. The school teacher who had replaced his daughter would be busy assembling the props for the program and seeing that the curtain would be pulled across the stage, which in reality was the altar. The teacher was a large, very plain Dutch woman, unmarried and actually not too old—but ugly as sin, Carl thought to himself.

Turning the last corner as they approached the church, the family passed a small graveyard where some of the ancestors on both sides of the family were buried. Too dark now to see any of the grave stones, Carl nonetheless envisioned some of the names that he had memorized over the years. He felt a sense of pride recalling that two of them, his grandfathers, had special markers commemorating their Civil War military service from 1861 to 1865.

The church was now in sight. It was ablaze with light. Several cars were parked at the side of the snowy road and two or three teams of horses were tied in front of the church. The excitement of the children, even the boy, was building fast. It was the most special of all nights of the year, the night of the Christmas program!

Carl soon recognized Doug's car and wondered if he by any chance had a bottle of whiskey. No, probably not. Carl evaluated the other cars and the buggies. He saw one or two that might have possibilities.

Hell, it was Christmas!

Chapter Eight

Carl was smart enough not to expect the warming days to last. It was April but he knew from experience that out of nowhere icy cold wind and even snow could come blasting across the fields. The last storm of the winter always seemed to be the most severe, one that the farmers re-lived the entire summer.

Carl glanced toward the orchard, a small plot of apple, cherry and pear trees growing on the other side of the chicken house. Any day now, the air would be filled with the wonderful aroma of their blossoms. The fruit never turned out to be much, perhaps because the kids picked and ate the green apples before they had a chance to ripen. The cherries were very sour and the pears usually a disappointment, but oh, how sweet the smell when the trees were in bloom.

On this mild Saturday, the little girls were searching for wild flowers. The wife had sent them to help at the new house by gathering pieces of wood and nails from what she hoped would soon be a nice yard. A nice yard with pretty flower beds and the blooming lilac tree that had survived the fire were very important to her. The girls had made a huge pile of end pieces of lumber at a sufficient distance from the house to light a fire. Sometimes the wife brought a cast iron skillet, homemade lard and potatoes to fry over the bonfire.

When they grew tired of gathering the wood and picking up nails, the girls asked if they could go down by the bridge to look for violets and Sweet William, the first flowers of spring. Carl assumed that the soil under the old red bridge and along the creek was somehow richer because that was the only place the wild flowers grew. Sometimes the girls would plot to surprise the Swede's mother by taking her a bouquet. Of course, the elderly lady could see them coming across the field, which spoiled the surprise but gave her time to pack a few homemade cookies in an empty coffee can in exchange for their thoughtfulness.

The house was shaping up nicely. Linoleum covered the kitchen floor and the cabinet tops. Carl cursed that the damn cabinets did not have doors. Nice shelves for the wife's dishes but no time now to stop to make the doors. It would take some special wood that had to be planed and sanded, which was tedious, to make the cabinet doors that he wanted. The kitchen had windows on the two outside walls that faced the south and west, and a door to the cement platform where the pump stood. The water from the deep well was so cold and so good that often truckers stopped to have a drink from the tin cup that hung on the pump. Best water in the county, they always said.

Carl sometimes wondered about his well water. Was it because of the strong smell of creosote that soaked the railroad ties, a half mile away? Or was it possible that the creosote had somehow seeped through the ground and into the well? He did not know if he could actually taste it in the water or if the smell was so strong on days when the wind blew from that direction that he imagined it. Carl did not want to dwell on his increasingly irritated stomach but could not help having vague doubts about the possibly polluted well water. Could there be any connection? He would look for something in the paper.

A cistern was also located on the west side of the house. Drain pipes from the eaves of the old house had kept it full of rain water that the wife used to wash their clothes. It was soft water, she said, which made it easier to get the clothes clean. Monday was usually the day for the washing, weather permitting, sometimes with bars of laundry soap that she had made with fat from butchered livestock and lye. She boiled the two together until it miraculously turned into soap. A soap called Ivory was available at the store when the wife thought she could afford it. Buckets of the rain water were drawn from the cistern and heated on an outside fire, then poured into a wash tub in the back yard. Piles of clothes were scrubbed on the wash board, rinsed in another tub of clean water, wrung as dry as possible and then hung with clothes pins on the line. There was never a fragrance quite like those clean clothes dried in the fresh air.

Carl smiled to himself thinking of the use he had made of the cistern on another occasion. He had gone to town with Doug and secretly brought home a quart of beer. He had put the brown bottle in a bucket and lowered it in the cistern to keep cool until he was alone to drink it. One of the girls must have been spying and reported it to the wife. Despite the uproar, Carl had taken the bottle to the barn and proceeded to drain it. Hell, a man had to have a drink once in a while.

His thoughts returning to the work at hand, Carl began nailing in place the base board that he had carefully sanded. Finishing the house in time for the wedding was the goal he had set for himself, and it would not be long now. Carl tried to imagine the living room full of people. The car of the bridegroom from Chicago would be in the front yard. The Chevy belonging to the second daughter's boyfriend, the dairy farmer would surely be there, too. The third daughter had recently met a young man who drove a Ford. The young man was said to be a crackerjack mechanic and seemed to care for the girl, whose eyesight was not good enough to get a job.

Carl could not see himself mingling with the wedding guests. He decided he would cross that bridge when the time came.

Chapter Nine

Again it was a nice day, but cool. The wife had reported that the temperature might reach sixty as he left that morning to work on the house. Still another day would be spent trying to finish the stairs on the south side of the living room. After struggling for several days Carl admitted in frustration that he could not do it alone. One problem was that directly below the stairs was an open section of flooring for the steps to the basement. How the hell? Stumped, Carl had sent word to his brother to come from Blakesville and lend a hand.

As he waited for the sound of his brother's car, he began sanding one of the nicely grained 12" x 40" boards spread before him on the floor. They would soon, with his brother's help, become the open stairway to the two bedrooms upstairs. With two maybe three coats of varnish, the staircase was to be the centerpiece of the entire house and the visible proof of his skill as a carpenter. Carl noticed that only about half dozen sheets of sand paper were left on hand. He wished to hell that he had asked his brother to bring a supply.

Carl thought for a while about not having a car. More neighbors were now getting automobiles. One of the damn fools had sneeringly suggested that Carl was afraid of machinery. Why else would he be plowing the field with a team of horses instead of a tractor? Carl pondered this statement, which he secretly conceded was partially true. But then, cars cost money; a new Ford V-8 was close to $400. He and the wife had six children, three of them still little kids. Hell, it cost money to raise a family. His brother had only two girls, while his younger sister and her husband, who also had a nice car, had none at all. Snooty bastards. His sister had been a nurse before she was married and her husband was what Carl called a gentleman farmer. No call for them to be stuck up. Hell, he was a carpenter and a damn good one, Carl thought, looking around at his progress.

He had not seen his younger sister since before the old house burned and wondered if they would be coming to the wedding. It was up to the wife to invite them if she wanted to, but he would have no part of it. Carl recalled the last time he had seen his younger sister. The wife had reported that they were invited to his sister's home for Sunday dinner. The little girls were excited about once again seeing their aunt's fancy house and furnishings. They had tantalized themselves wondering if there would be pie, cake or some delicious pudding for dessert. If pudding, it might be butterscotch or chocolate, or possibly custard, which was their third choice.

It had taken half the morning to bundle everyone into the wagon and the other half to make the trip across the county. But almost immediately upon their arrival, his sister, known for her unreasonable temper, began to berate him for some old perceived insult. The sister's husband stood meekly to one side during his wife's tirade, while the girls looked longingly at the hot dishes arrayed on the table. What the hell? He looked at the wife for direction. She silently took the children's arms, leading them back to the wagon. Off toward home they went, empty stomachs and all. Worse still, the team of horses had not had time for a drink at the water tank. Christ! He wished he had stood up to her, as he usually did. Normally, the fights she started could go on for hours, even days, each ugly outburst gaining momentum with sufficient time to think of additional damning words. To hell with her.

Carl had one brother and two sisters. His older sister, the opposite of the younger one who was a hellion, loved to entertain his girls. She too had no children of her own, but had a wonderful humorous husband who loved to have them visit. Their uncle would sneak them into the front room that was rarely used. He showed them how to play records on the Victorola while his wife cooked whatever was on hand. She was not much of a cook and sometimes it was only potatoes, gravy and biscuits, but it was always a treat. Carl reflected on what a shame it was to see the girls' aunt and uncle so seldom. After all, they lived in the same county.

Carl heard the car slow down to cross the bridge and finally come into sight around the barn. His brother took his time getting out, gathering the tools that he had placed on the floor board. Carl smelled the strong odor of whiskey, but observed that his brother did not appear affected by it as they approached the dilemma of the stairs. After a brief consultation, the two brothers took up their hammers and the stairs soon began to take shape. They shared a laugh that neither one had fallen into the basement. Carl loved his brother. What a shame that whiskey seemed to have taken over his life, and that was not just the wife talking. Still, the man was a hell of a carpenter.

When the sun was directly overhead, Carl heard the wife approaching from the direction of the railroad. She was singing a song she had learned from the girls. When they came home from time to time before the house burned, the oldest girl would bring her banjo. At night they would sit in the yard and play and sing *"Danny Boy"*, *"Mexicali Rose"*, Carl's favorite *"Wagon Wheels"* and other popular songs they had heard on the radio. There was some talk that a radio station would soon be opening in town. The only radio stations Carl could get were WHO-Des Moines or WGN-Chicago. About all they were good for was to play the same damn music over and over or to give baseball scores. Carl liked Dutch Reagan, the sports announcer on WHO-Des Moines, but he still preferred the newspaper that covered a wide variety of news and subjects in which Carl was intensely interested.

The wife was carrying a basket covered with a clean dish cloth. As agreed the night before, she had left the boy in the care of the third daughter who had returned to live at home. The wife was bringing dinner as thanks for his brother's help. Carl and his brother washed up at the pump while she spread the cloth and arranged their dinner of boiled eggs, sweet apple sauce generously flavored with cinnamon and a loaf of fresh-baked bread. The wife looked suspicious at the smell of whiskey but did not comment, since she had sniffed and determined that Carl had not shared the bottle that was always in his brother's car.

After driving a few more nails and delivering instructions on how to finish the stairs, Carl's brother started the car and drove away. Carl soon heard the thwack, thump as it went over the bridge.

Realizing that he had a rare moment alone with the wife, Carl held her close, taking care that his stubble of beard did not chafe her face. After all these years, her face was still smooth and soft. Once he had found a jar of Pond's Cold Cream on top of the bureau and began to curse at her spendthrift ways, until she told him it was a gift from the girls. Christ, he loved her so much but did not know how to tell her, and he could do so little to repay her goodness.

Finally she asked if the Indian blanket that was kept in the barn needed to be taken home to be washed. No one knew why it was called the Indian blanket; certainly it had never belonged to any Indians. However, it did have a colorful although faded design and was strong and warm. Several times after he had begun building the house, the wife had brought his noon meal and afterward they had lain on the Indian blanket that covered a pile of hay in the loft of the barn. Carl read her thoughts when she asked about the blanket but felt fatigue and weakness wash over him. It was too late. No use. Not any more.

Chapter Ten

His tallest ladder stood against the side of the house and Carl was on the top rung. He was trying to decide whether to build soffits under the eaves. Another pending decision was lightning rods. All the older houses had lightning rods on the roof but Carl felt they were not worth the time and money. Hell, lightning could strike a tree and the wind could carry the sparks to the roof. However, the shingles that Carl had selected were asbestos and were not supposed to burn. Pausing for a moment in his decision-making, Carl inspected the roofing job and decided that it was a job well done. Not only looked damn good but the roof was tight as a drum. Carl did not look forward to painting the house as much as he had enjoyed the actual carpentry. A primer coat had been applied to the siding in preparation for the paint, which like it or not had to be done.

Looking down to his left, Carl saw the garden from a new perspective. The wife and girls had spent several Saturdays planting vegetables before school was out for the summer. The young tender leaves of lettuce and the white and red radishes were long gone, the lettuce served with homemade buttermilk dressing and the radishes sliced between pieces of crusty bread. The potato plants were blooming. Later in the fall, the potatoes would be dug and stored in a bin in the new basement. A bucket or two would be saved for planting next spring. The wife knew exactly how deep to dig the holes for the girls to place the pieces of potato they had carefully carved. Each piece had to have an eye in order to grow into a new plant.

The grape vines that grew along the side of the garden nearest the road were a healthy dark green. The grapes looked a little dusty to Carl but it didn't stop the kids from helping themselves until their hands and cheeks were covered with purple juice. Carl had decided to make grape wine in the basement of the new house once the wedding was over. A man in Blakesville had a supply of bottles and corks and had shared the recipe. Carl knew the wife would object to the wine and especially to the amount of sugar that it would take but what the hell. This time he was determined to win the argument.

In the total stillness of the morning Carl heard a car, maybe more than one, coming along the road. He was perplexed when the motors were turned off before they reached the bridge. Descending the ladder, he decided to investigate. Carl did not walk down the road but headed through the field to a high spot on the creek bank. The nightly shortcut where he crossed the creek to reach the railroad track was upstream a short distance. As the creek neared the bridge, it flowed into a round pond-like area that had been excavated years before by the railroad company. For as long as Carl could remember, it was called the swimming hole. His two oldest daughters had learned to swim in it and the surrounding grassy area was a popular spot for family picnics. Although it was on his land, Carl had no objection to neighbors and vacationers using it for picnics and camping. In fact, no one ever bothered to ask permission as the swimming hole was considered open to the public. There was only one lake in a far corner of the county, too far for many people. Neither Carl nor any member of his family had ever made the trip. Why should they? They had their own swimming hole and picnic grounds.

Carl's confusion deepened at what he saw from the creek bank. Two cars that he did not recognize were parked side by side near the road. Instead of families unpacking picnic baskets, Carl saw two men in black suits, several women and girls in white dresses and some young boys of about nine or ten years of age wearing white shirts. They proceeded to the water's edge with bowed heads and clasped hands. Carl could not make out the words of the hymn that they sang, but it sounded like "Shall We Gather at the River". One of the men began to pray. As he continued to call on God in a loud voice, the other man carried each child into the water, clothing and all, and completely immersed them. Carl felt panic when he saw their little heads go under water while the man he assumed was a preacher prayed on. Carl himself was afraid of the water and had never attempted learning to swim. Next, the man led each woman into the creek. Could this be a baptism? Carl had heard of a church in Blakesville where people were placed in water to cleanse them from sin. What the hell? When all had been immersed and returned to dry land, the strident praying continued. Carl turned and hurried back to the house without waiting for further developments. Shaken, he eventually heard the cars start up and drive away.

Carl found it difficult to regain his concentration. To begin with, the house as sketched on the blueprints was built. What remained were details such as the painting and some of the trim. Carl tried to focus on which to tackle first, but for once he was indecisive. He leaned against the tree in the front yard and let his mind wander to the farm and not just the house on it. Carl did not understand the ritual that he had just witnessed but was pleased that the participants had chosen his swimming hole. His gaze fell on a pasture across the road where the Boy Scouts camped some summers. The girls called it the Garden of Eden. They had names for other spots: the crossroads, the billy place, the big pasture, the little pasture, the lane, the bottom field, the big hill. Carl had to admit that all of them from the oldest to the youngest appeared to love the place; the farm that was a millstone around his neck was home to them.

The date for the wife and kids to move into the new house was set. A couple of neighbors with wagons were lined up to move the household goods from the rented house to the new. He and the wife would have the upstairs bedroom on the west and the three youngest would be on the other side. The third daughter would have the downstairs bedroom. Carl stopped to wonder why he did not feel excitement at the thought of the house being occupied. It had been his solitary domain for so long and he was not sure it was good enough yet for the wife and kids. But hell, Carl thought, he would be relieved of some of the work when the rest of the family was around. The wife was expert at milking cows and one of the chores the girls liked best was pumping water into the trough. The horses had always run to the water trough when he came in from plowing, but the cattle liked to drink from the creek. Damn fools, Carl thought. He had to admit that he did not understand livestock.

Again Carl felt that he must get busy. He needed to have a hammer in his hand, accomplishing something that he could see. This morning's religious scene was distracting him. Carl wondered why he had begun to sing *"The Old Rugged Cross"* when he thought he was dying, and why had he thanked God when he survived. Why was he uneasy when he was in the church and looked up at the portrait of Jesus? Could it be guilt that when he attended church all those years ago he was only thinking of getting the wife into his buggy? Christ Almighty! But wait. Could it be that he cursed and took the name of God in vain so often, so regularly and so angrily? Hell's fire! This kind of thinking was disturbing.

Carl knew that someday he would have to *get right with God*, an expression he had heard used by the preachers on the radio. But for now, he needed to finish this damn house.

Chapter Eleven

Carl stood in the doorway of the barn and surveyed his handiwork. The house was as finished as it was going to be.

He had given it two coats of white paint. All three outside doors had glass panes, which the wife had washed with vinegar and water and dried with old rags until they sparkled. The stoop at the front door had several steps but no hand rails, which Carl had decided were unnecessary. He was satisfied that the eight foot by eight foot cement square at the back door provided a nice access to the kitchen. The water pump was situated in the cement; thus, a minimum of water and mud would be tracked onto the linoleum. A new green enamel cook stove sat in one corner of the kitchen. It would burn either wood or cobs and had a roomy oven. A round oak table, large enough for the entire family, was placed under the window to the left of the back door. The kitchen cabinets did not have doors, but what the hell, Carl thought.

No heating stove was necessary in any of the rooms, since the shiny new coal-burning furnace had been installed in the basement and was ready to go.

Carl was pleased with the living room. As he had envisioned so many times, the open stairs that had been sanded and re-sanded gleamed with several coats of varnish. A small window at the bottom of the stairway shed light in that corner of the room. The little girls had already found that it was a good spot in the evening to watch for car lights on the other side of the bridge, which might mean company was coming. Despite the anticipation, they were usually disappointed when the cars went on by.

The wood flooring also shone with varnish and floor polish, and the Duncan Phyfe table was just right. As planned, it sat under a window on the north side of the room. The two older girls and the wife had asked Doug for a ride to town to pick out new furniture, which cost nearly $300. It had taken the girls a long time to save so much. The three of them had shed a few tears when it was delivered.

Each of the two upstairs bedrooms had a new bed and dresser and the downstairs bedroom was also furnished. Not much had accumulated since the fire, so moving into the house had been simple. The two youngest girls liked to tell the story of the first day they came home from school to the new house. They were hungry as usual but the only food in the house was a loaf of bread and a jar of mustard. Nonetheless, they made a mustard sandwich, which they said was delicious.

Several storms that brought hard rain had swept through the area, but the roof had not leaked and the seal around the windows remained tight. Carl had checked carefully for loose or missing shingles or any other signs of damage, but all appeared to be intact. The house was strong.

From his vantage point in the upper door of the barn, Carl waited for the cars to arrive from the wedding. He had declined to attend with the excuse that he had no suitable clothes. The girls had argued that they would buy him a suit but he refused. However, he had shaved and wore a clean shirt with his overalls.

Carl recalled his younger days and the good clothes he had worn to that same church where this evening's wedding was held. What had changed him in little more than twenty-five years? Carl could not recall the last time he had laughed out loud. He had been amused at times in the past when he and Doug had gone to town or at little things the kids had done, but it had been a long time. Carl suspected that he had been sick for a while but also knew that he had no choice but to keep going. The wife and kids deserved to live in a nice house. That single thought had driven him since the day the old house burned.

The first car rumbled over the bridge down the road. Soon it appeared around the side of the barn and turned into the yard, parking to one side of the lawn to make room for the other cars. It was the Chevy, full of grown-ups and the kids. Soon lamps were lit and Carl could picture the second girl setting out the dainty plates of food she had prepared that morning. Two leaves had been put in the Duncan Phyfe table that had been pulled into the middle of the living room. The Ford came around the barn, and another car was right behind. Clouds of dust rose from the road. Carl recognized Doug's car and knew that he would soon head for the barn. At that moment, Carl decided that he would not join the party. He felt sure that the new son-in-law would bring him a drink of whiskey, if any was available. He recalled hearing the wife speak against having any whiskey on hand for the occasion, but the more worldly couple from Chicago may have overruled her.

Carl was happy to stay where he was because he could get a better view of the house. It looked nice with the light shining through the windows and people moving about inside. He recalled the day he had mixed the cement for the basement floor. Carl then relived each step, the shiny nails, the smell of new lumber, each day's accomplishment, and there the house stood before him, finished. He tried not to think of the painful walks up the track each night. Instead, he considered those trips simply a brief pause before the next day's rewarding tasks. It was all behind him now.

Hard as he tried, Carl could not imagine going back to his life as a farmer, not for long anyway. Hell, he was a carpenter.

Epilogue

Carl Todd McElroy died at 8:20 p.m., Friday, February 5, 1937. He was 53 years old.

After attending a square dance at the home of a neighbor, Carl decided to walk home alone without his family. Taking a short cut across a hilly pasture, he slid on the ice into a deep ditch and fractured his hip. His calls for help were heard by his wife and children who rode home in the car of the loyal friend mentioned in this story. Three or four men were summoned to carry Carl to the house. They made a gurney and had to remove their shoes to navigate the icy incline in their stocking feet.

Someone went to the home of a neighbor who had a telephone. A hearse was called to transport Carl to the hospital. He was diagnosed as having pneumonia and died several days later. No tests were available to determine if cancer or some other disease may have contributed to his ill health or his death.

One of the hymns at Carl's funeral, held at the First Methodist Church in Ottumwa, Iowa, was *"The Old Rugged Cross"*.

The house that Carl built so lovingly survived until the late fall of 1969. On a snowy night, with the tenants away, the house burned to the ground. Cause of the fire was unknown.

Who Held His Hand

(a poem written by the "third daughter" after her father's death)

His life was uneventful;
The money that he did not have
Lies still within the rich, black earth
Upon his widow's farm.

His talents were not those of skill;
His art decays, discovered not
His eyes can roam no more along the waving wheat,
Upon the shooting corn,
High to the fluttering pigeons on the barn.

His love was not romantic;
He ate her meals without applause—without a pause
For tenderness. He drove his herd to pasture,
A hickory lash within his hand.

His soul was not religious.
He cursed without a worry.
He spat between his teeth,
Avoiding beyond hope, the church upon the hill.
Though still,
A little child forever trotted after him.
A little hand relaxing often in his grimy paw.

Atimes his face would break from stony silence
Into a rhapsody of smile—and then some age-old hymn might
Burst from his bewhiskered jaw.
His land he tilled with horse and plow
And no one ever knew his dreams.

But now that he is gone—it seems
That horse and plow and child and sod
Were art and love and hope, and God
Was not so far away.
Has come to me a strange new thought, this day;
I loved him so, as few, I understand;
I was a little child who held his hand.

—by Kathryn Eleanor Whitaker

Good Morning

(Another poem, written by the "third granddaughter"
seventy years after her grandfather's death—the generations of
cousins have over the years been drawn to their rural roots)

I don't remember exactly how it was
But the breeze always brings
Some memory of those mornings.

Where I live, it is hot—almost always
But some mornings bring with them
A sweet coolness and movement.

Then, we sat out with weak coffee,
Shelling beans, shucking corn, sharing time
Family separated, but together for a while.

Vacationers all—
They from living in the same place with others gone,
We from the separation of miles.

Iowa summers, cool mornings, aunts, uncles, cousins, accents
And always the breeze . . .
Blowing softly and fresh.
Today will be hot, it is August
But it is morning—and a breeze brings
A cool memory of then and there and them.

—by Mary Elizabeth Speyrer